Mary

Four Weeks with the Mother of Jesus

Edited by
**Wolfgang Bader and
Stephen Liesenfeld**

Foreword by
Robert F. Morneau

New City Press
Hyde Park, New York

Published in the United States by New City Press
202 Cardinal Rd., Hyde Park, NY 12538
www.newcitypress.com
©2008 New City Press (English translation)

Translated by Edward Hagmann from the original German edition
Maria: Vier Wochen mit der Mutter Jesu
©2006 Neue Stadt, Munich, Germany

Cover design by Durva Correia

Library of Congress Cataloging-in-Publication Data:
Maria. English
   Mary : four weeks with the Mother of Jesus / edited by Wolfgang Bader
and Stefan Liesenfeld ; foreword by Robert F. Morneau.
       p. cm.
   Includes bibliographical references.
   ISBN 978-1-56548-281-4 (pbk. : alk. paper)   1. Mary, Blessed Virgin,
Saint--Meditations.   I. Bader, Wolfgang.   II. Liesenfeld, Stephen.

BT608.5.M366 2008
232.91--dc22   2007028750

Printed in the United States of America

Contents

three
Mary and Others

four
Mary and Us

Foreword

In recent years, numerous books have been published dealing with the lives of the saints. Indeed, they are most welcome, for we need mentors and models on this perilous human journey we all travel. And surely, Mary, the Mother of our Savior, stands at the top of the list as someone who both teaches and witnesses the path of discipleship. To enter more deeply into the mind and heart of Mary is to enter into the realm of grace, for she was filled with God's light, love, and life.

In this meditative work (for it is not a book to be "read" but rather "prayed"), we are given passages from scripture, quotations from various spiritual writers, as well as reflections by this volume's two editors, Wolfgang Bader and Stephen Liesenfeld. The methodology is invitational, suggesting that the reader/pray-er spend a portion of each day in a four week period pondering Mary's relationship with God, with her Son, with others, and with us.

The aim of this small volume is not an increase in theological knowledge, though that may happen. Rather, the intent is growth in understanding and appreciating Mary's role in the Christian life. She basically did two things: she obeyed and she gave herself away. This obedience and self-giving is at the heart of the Eucharist. Mary lived that life; she lived it to the full.

One of the great lessons Mary teaches us is the instruction she gave the waiters at the wedding feast of Cana. Her words should be etched on our hearts: "Do whatever he tells you" (Jn 2:5b). Do we dare add to Mary's imperative? "Do [with joy] whatever he tells you." The tone of Mary's life was one of trust and joy. That is why her life magnified the Lord and why she rejoiced in all that the Lord did for her.

A warning! Pondering this book in a prayerful manner may lead to a personal transformation. If such is the case, throw caution to the wind.

Bishop Robert F. Morneau

Mary
and God

one

Chosen

The mother of Jesus holds a special fascination for many people. She was and is celebrated in song, and venerated even outside Christianity. People you would not expect feel drawn to her, have a relationship with her. There is a kind of poetry about Mary and her association with her Son. Werner Bergengruen says of children that they possess the aura of creation before the fall, still undefiled, a suggestion of the early morning and purity of the beginning. Many find this again in the mother of Jesus. The words of Scripture apply also and especially to her:

"God chose us in Christ
before the foundation of the world,
to be holy and blameless before him ...
to the praise of his glorious grace
that he freely bestowed on us
in the Beloved."

(Ephesians 1:4–6)

We are not products of chance. We are willed and loved by God, with our special gifts and tasks. Mary's unique task was to be the mother of Jesus.

Her life shows from the very beginning the mark of God who thought of her and chose her, who burst into her existence, who demanded much of her and always accompanied her. Nor are we simply thrown into the world and then left to ourselves. We are not alone in our (often futile) attempt to live as "holy and blameless." Again and again God's glorious grace, his kindness and compassion, surround us and capture us. He wants to give us again the unsullied beauty that was ours in the beginning.

"I am grateful that in Mary,
the handmaid of the Lord,
I can imagine what God had in mind
when he created human beings.
I am glad that I can see redemption
in a gift without blemish,
in humanity healed at its root."

(Klaus Hemmerle)

2 Spoken To

God speaks to humans through angels. In the Bible there is often something overwhelming about their appearance. Their brightness blinds, their appearance frightens.

The angel came to Zechariah, father of John the Baptist, as he was carrying out his morning priestly service in the temple and offering incense (Lk 1:8–11). With Mary it was different. As if it were quite natural, the angel Gabriel entered her living room softly and on tiptoe. God did not wait for Mary to come to him in the sanctuary; he came to her for a visit. The angel entered Mary's room and said, "Greetings; rejoice!" (Lk 1:28).

"Greetings!" Using the same word the angel spoke to Mary, Jesus turned to the women who came to his tomb after his resurrection (see Mt 28:9). The first greeting marked the beginning of God's unusual conversation with Mary. The second greeting marked the beginning of the risen Lord's never-ending presence among us: "I am with you always, to the end of the age" (Mt 28:20).

God wants to be near us: he greets us, or conveys his greetings (if we can put it that way) through others. As he spoke to Mary through an angel, so we should know that we are greeted and spoken to by him.

And when we greet Mary with the angel's word, it is "a thank-you to the loving God" who "gave her to us as a sign of his nearness" *(Joseph Ratzinger)*.

"Hail Mary, full of grace,
the Lord is with you…."
He is with you because he also
wished to be with us in your Child,
who is with us always,
until the end of time.
He spoke to you,
in order to speak to us words of comfort
through his Son, your Child,
Jesus of Nazareth.

3 Favored and Troubled

The angel said to Mary: "You are divinely favored, Mary, the Lord is with you" (Lk 1:28). Favor — *cháris* in Greek — means goodwill, grace, God's loving kindness. Mary does not have God's favor or goodwill *of* herself, it was given to her for free. Neither does she have it *for* herself, but rather in view of her vocation and task, which is to become the mother of Jesus.

The greatest and most important thing in life is given us as a gift. God is good to us, not because *we* have been good, but because *he* is good! Here we touch on something of the secret of Jesus' mother. She lived centered on God, on his love and his promise: "I am with you!" Mary stands in the long line of those to whom God spoke these marvelous words, in the host of great Old Testament figures, from Isaac, Jacob and Moses all the way to the little and unknown ones among her people.

Mary "was much perplexed at the angel's words and pondered what sort of greeting this might be" (Lk 1:29). Who am I that you are speaking to me? What about this child whose mother I am to be? What is your plan? Don't you know anything about me and my limitations?

It can be troubling when God speaks to someone, when through an angel, people, or circumstances God entrusts a person with a task — and believes the person capable of doing it!

"Sometimes we would like to run away from our task. We would like to have our peace.… And yet for us also Mary's way lies open.… Very quietly, the angel comes into the room of our life. My humanity, broken and in peril, is also called into God's favor, stands under the sign of that loving yes that God is speaking.… Come, have courage, courage to be a human being, courage as great as God's — you are not alone! Jesus goes before you, Mary goes with you."

(Klaus Hemmerle)

4 Free to Question

The angel tried to alleviate Mary's fear: "Do not be afraid, Mary, for you have found favor with God. And now, you will conceive in your womb and bear a son, and you will name him Jesus."

For Mary it must have been a tremendous moment. Tremendously great. And incomprehensible: "Mary said to the angel, 'How can this be, since I am a virgin?' " (Lk 1:30–34).

Mary did not refuse. But she asked, "How can this be?" In this "how" she brings her God-given reason into play. She would like to understand.

God allows us human beings the freedom to ask, to inquire, to "question our way" into his plans.

"Mary appears here,
not as a blindly submissive subject,
but as the free daughter of God
who asks the Father for
an explanation.
She is far from being
a timidly submissive woman
or one whose piety
was repellent to others."

(Pope Paul VI)

God seeks conversation.
Not just with Mary.
Let us ask,
let us contribute with heart and mind,
with our reservations and doubts,
with our beliefs.
Whether and how God answers —
that, of course, we must leave to him.

5 A Momentous Yes

The angel answered Mary: "The Holy Spirit will come upon you and the power of the Most High will overshadow you; therefore the child to be born will be holy; he will be called Son of God.... Then Mary said, 'Here I am, the servant of the Lord; let it be with me according to your word' " (Lk 1:35–38).

Mary's response is the most momentous, the most decisive yes in the history of the world.

Mary's yes comes, not from just an enthusiastic and joyful heart, but from her whole heart, soul, mind and powers. These powers are not her own: "This is what the angel is obviously thinking, too; therefore the power of the Holy Spirit must overshadow her.... To become nothing, only an instrument, while believing so strongly, is absolutely beyond a human being's powers, even more than the supreme effort of one's last bit of strength."

(Sören Kierkegaard)

"On a certain day,
when the time was fulfilled
and the waiting period had passed,
God approached a pure virgin.
He knocked softly on the door.
He asked if he might live
and dwell in the house of humans.
And Mary accepted
because there was room in her inn.
The Word became flesh in the virgin's
    womb,
and the divine life began to grow in
    the world."

(Leonardo Boff)

"When Mary learned
that the Lord was calling her,
she said her yes.
Never again did she take it back.
Her whole life was a constant yes.
Our life, too, must become this one
    word, yes.
Holiness is a lived yes to God.
We let God take from us whatever he
    wants,
and we promise to accept joyfully
all that he gives us."

(Mother Teresa)

6 Back to Everyday Life

"Then the angel departed from her" (Lk 1:38).

The angel left Mary's room as quietly as he had entered. This is a special moment in her life. What does she do? She sets out for her cousin Elizabeth, the woman in whom, as the angel said, God had also done impossible things.

We, too, are sometimes touched by an angel, by light, fortune, favor, by a call. It can happen that we stop there, that we would like to cling to these moments. But the point is to "mix in" what was with what is happening — like yeast in the flour of our everyday relationships, like light in that which is dark or grey.

After the angel left, everyday life went on for Mary, but for her it was no longer just daily life. A new life had begun. Perhaps she spoke to the child in her womb, questioned him about the incredible thing. Where are you from? What should I tell the others?

From now on Mary's life could no longer be separated from her Son's life. In life *for* her child, in life *with* her child, she lived for and with God.

"It is fine to honor Mary
as virgin and Mother of God,
but we can also call her Mary of the
   dishes,
the broom and the cooking pots.
She washed the dishes,
cooked dinner and scrubbed the floor.
She did nothing extraordinary,
but she did the ordinary things in an
   extraordinary way.
She did what everyone does,
   but in union with her Son Jesus.
   We can do that too!"

(Albino Luciani)

7 Mother of God

Mary's divine motherhood means that God has made the lowly virgin great. To be sure, Mary remains a creature of God, the "beloved daughter of the Father," as the Council puts it (*Lumen Gentium* 53), but God called her to be mother of his Son. God made Mary great by making himself lowly. Such is God's love.

God gave Mary the gift to be able to give God to the world. God accepts Mary's gift, her humanity, her yes. He accepts her as the root from which "he can grow into our history, from below and from within" *(Klaus Hemmerle).*

"All her glory has been summed up in a single word: she is called Mother of God. No one can say anything greater of her or to her, even if one had as many tongues as there are leaves on the trees, or grass in the fields, or stars in the sky, or sand by the sea. It needs to be pondered in the heart what it means to be Mother of God."

(Martin Luther)

Or as Bariona, the "singer of street ballads" in Sartre's Christmas play of the same name, says: "I think there are … moments, rapid and fleeting, when Mary feels *simultaneously* that Christ is her Son, her little child, and that he is God. She looks at him and thinks: 'This God is my child. This divine flesh is my flesh. He is made of me, he has my eyes and this shape of his mouth is the shape of mine. He looks like me. He is God and he looks like me.' And no woman has had her God for herself alone in that way. A little God one can hold in one's arms and shower with kisses, a warm God who smiles and breathes, a God one can touch and who lives. And it is in one of those moments that I would paint Mary, if I were a painter…."

two

Mary and *Her Son*

A Mystery

A child is a miracle. Many, probably most mothers and fathers experience this to some degree or other. This has nothing to do with romantic star-gazing. Sitting up nights or changing wet diapers makes one immune to daydreaming. Children need very concrete and sometimes very demanding care. Yet a child remains a miracle. It demands reverence. (How easily we forget that every human being — whatever that person has become — remains this miraculous, amazing child!)

Mary, too, wrapped her child in diapers. She knows about life. But at the same time she knows about the miraculous. Like other mothers. And yet quite different. The angel's words hang over her relationship with her child like a great mystery.

"Mary's attitude was determined by the angel's message. That message had become the living, increasingly active, ever developing and deepening center of her life. Because of it, her relationship with her Son was kept from ever descending to the merely human. Whatever he was and spoke and did, she had to apply to what she had experienced at that time.

"This did not call into question her maternal relationship. Living together with her Son, Mary did and experienced everything a mother does and experiences. On the other hand, Jesus was the Son of God and as such exceeded every merely human possibility. She was still unable to realize the true importance of this fact....

"According to the angel's word, Mary was 'blessed among women,' full of the possibilities of holy insight, love and intimacy. Yet she remained a human being, really and truly. So, in her relationship with her Son there must have been, in the midst of the deepest intimacy, a distance, a failure to understand, which is also revealed in the narrative...."

(Romano Guardini)

2 What Shall Become of Him?

Shepherds came to Bethlehem to see the child. "They found Mary and Joseph, and the child lying in the manger. When they saw this, they made known what had been told them about this child; and all who heard it were amazed at what the shepherds told them. But Mary treasured all these words and pondered them in her heart" (Lk 2:15–19). The Greek word for "ponder" (*symbállein* — our word "symbol" also derives from it) means to go over something in one's mind in order to classify it, to try to interpret something that is not clear. Mary was looking for the "connection," trying to classify the events and the things said in the context of her whole life, thoughts and feelings. The others are "amazed" at the things said, but Mary goes over them, thinks seriously about them, ponders them. What will become of the child — and of her as well?

For the mother of a newborn, the child is the center of attention. This is also and especially true for Mary. She observes the events and tries to understand them. Angels and people she did not invite rejoice and praise her son. Heaven and

earth are looking at him. Mary will do everything
for her newborn, and she begins to sense that her
place will be at his side.

"Happy and painful incidents,
complex historical events
are kept by Mary in her heart
and connected to each other
so that their deeper
meaning might become clear....
We too need the ability today
to discern the deeper
meaning and connection
in the many different things
that are happening,
whether dark or bright,
clear or incomprehensible."

(Carlo Maria Martini)

3 Who Learns from Whom?

The interplay between teaching and learning shapes the relationship between parents and children more than one might think. Children and parents grow and mature together and with each other.

When God's Son became a human being in Mary, he made himself a learner. A reversal of roles that turns upside down our conventional ways of thinking. Does this perhaps mean that not only teaching but also learning can be divine? We like to teach. To learn how to learn, to let ourselves be shown other new things ... this is also a form of doing what God does, for "what counts is not how much we know but how much we love" *(Thérèse of Lisieux)*.

"Mary will have to do both things at once: introduce her child into the business of being human (and this does not mean merely teaching him how to walk and speak, but also introducing him to the religion of his fathers) and learn steadily more from her child how one behaves as a child of God."

(Hans Urs von Balthasar)

"Nazareth is a kind of school
where we may begin
to discover what Christ's life was
like and even to understand his
    Gospel....
How wonderful to be close to Mary,
learning again the lesson
of the true meaning of life,
learning again God's truths....
First we learn from its silence....
Second, we learn about family life.
May Nazareth serve as a model
of what the family should be.
May it show us the family's
holy and enduring character
and exemplify its basic function in
    society:
a community of love and sharing,
beautiful for the problems it poses
and the rewards its brings....
Finally, in Nazareth ...
we learn about work
and the discipline it entails."

(Pope Paul VI in Nazareth)

4 Incomprehensible Maturity

"**M**ary constantly experienced how her Son was pulling away from her. Especially important, therefore, are those episodes in which an action on the part of Jesus makes the separation between himself and her explicit.... They distinctly highlight what was becoming a constant: Jesus was incomprehensible. But she accepted this incomprehensibility in her life. She put up with it and even grew in that regard. Once again the characteristic feature of Mary's attitude appears. Her faith remains steadfast in incomprehensibility, waiting for light from God....

"She believes in something incomprehensible, something that is to come. She grows in this faith, and this growth has a Christian meaning and beauty that no exceptional circumstances could equal. During the long years of life in Nazareth, during the period of Jesus' public activity, and during the fruitfulness of the last days, she grows to a maturity into which the Pentecost event entered."

(Romano Guardini)

The First Disciple

During the approximately three years in which Jesus passed through many Palestinian villages and cities, his mother was also with him at times, along with the disciples he had chosen and the women who aided and assisted him.

At a wedding in Cana, to which Mary, Jesus and the disciples had been invited, his mother had a keen grasp of an awkward situation. She pointed out to her Son that the wine was running short.

One day a woman addressed Jesus from the crowd: "Blessed is the womb that bore you and the breasts that nursed you." Jesus replied: "Blessed rather are those who hear the word of God and obey it" (see Lk 11:27–28).

What mattered most to Jesus was to show that his Father was the center of his life. His mother belonged to the group of those who, like he himself, hear God's word and pattern their life on it. She was, as Pope Paul VI put it, "the first and most perfect disciple of Christ."

"Women today see Mary
as she is portrayed in Scripture:
as a mother with a Son
whose vocation causes
her pain and uncertainty,
and as a companion of Jesus
on a way where she must learn
that he accepts as brother,
sister and mother
everyone who does
the will of his Father.
They meet Mary beneath the cross
with the women
who remain near Jesus
while the men flee.
For women today Mary is
Jesus' partner in his work of salvation,
co-bearer of his burden."

(Waltraud Herbstrith)

Beneath the Cross of Her Son 6

Mary had accompanied Jesus along many ways. From the beginning she had experienced that it was a dangerous way. Love is vulnerable and helpless (since it cannot demand an answer) if it is not understood and accepted. The way of Jesus, who had preached and practiced nothing but love, led to the cross — out of love "for you and for many," as he himself put it the night before he died.

In this most bitter hour many abandon him; a few watch from a distance. According to the Gospel of John, the only ones standing beneath the cross are his aunt, two women named Mary (the wife of Clopas and Mary Magdalene), one of his disciples and his mother. Jesus entrusted his mother to the disciple whom he especially loved. He was to take her into his home as his mother.

We can only guess what was going through Mary's mind during these moments. Again and again Mary must have learned that God's ways are mysterious. His love for humanity transcends and goes beyond all understanding, all imagination.

Stabat Mater. Mary persevered, she remained there beside her crucified Son.

"Mary beneath the cross,
who says yes
to the sacrifice of her Son,
is for me virtue personified.
She, the Mother of Sorrows,
the one we call the *Desolata*,
can be our mentor
in the practice of self-denial....
She shows us what it means to lose,
to be able to let go."

(Chiara Lubich)

Forever Joined

Mary and her risen Son

"What did you feel, Mary,
when Magdalene said to you
that she had seen Jesus in the garden?
And when Peter and John
came running to you,
to tell you how they had seen the
    empty tomb … ?
What does it mean to believe
that Jesus has risen from the dead?
Did you see him again those days?
The Gospel says nothing about you….
Why didn't he appear to you … ?
Was Jesus referring to you
when he said to Thomas,
'Blessed are those who do not see and
    yet believe'?
Were you perhaps the only one who
    had no need
to see in order to believe?
And you were blessed. I believe it was so.
For that reason you are our master in
    faith,

and Elizabeth's tribute to you,
at the very beginning,
was the greatest praise anyone can
    bestow on you:
'Blessed are you because you have
    believed.'
You had no need to see for yourself,
with your own eyes.
You believed in your risen Son,
and that was enough for you."

(Carlo Carretto)

The close connection between mother and Son remains beyond the death of the Son. And also beyond the death of the mother.

We have no information about Mary's last days. In his last prayer to his Father, Jesus said: "I desire that those also, whom you have given me, may be with me where I am" (Jn 17:24).

These words were applied to Mary very early on. No one can believe that the love that had bound Jesus and Mary would end with death. Mary, the mother who had welcomed Christ into her body and into her life, embodies the hope that life with Jesus is something lasting.

three

Mary and Others

Mary and Joseph

It had begun so beautifully. Mary, a young girl in Nazareth, was engaged by her parents to be married, as was the custom at the time. Joseph, her husband-to-be, had a good reputation. He was regarded as a devout and upright man. The two were probably hoping they could marry soon, for they wanted children. And then came Mary's unexpected conversation with the angel. The young woman from Nazareth gave God her yes. Joseph stood aside. To avoid greater harm, he decided to release Mary from the marriage contract and to separate from her. At that moment God began a personal saga with him also. The angel of the Lord told him he should not dismiss Mary but take her to himself. The child was not from another man but from the Holy Spirit. Joseph too gave his yes. He did "as the angel of the Lord had commanded him" (Mt 1:24). He did the same later, according to Matthew's account, when he took the child and mother and fled to Egypt, in order to save the child from being murdered by Herod's henchmen.

By means of a "detour" (and may the detour have been the shortest path?) the two individual paths of Mary and Joseph became a single new shared path. From Klaus Hemmerle comes the evocative statement:

"God disrupts
and in this way binds together."

Like Mary, Joseph is also among the disciples who put God's word into practice, who fulfill God's will and so are called blessed by Jesus.

The unusual story of Mary and Joseph shows that each individual yes to God creates a deep bond that sustains the marital relationship and family life, including one's relationship with the children ... and with the child called Jesus.

"May it be done to me according to your word."

Joseph did "as the angel of the Lord had commanded him."

2 Mary and Elizabeth

Mary was entrusted by the angel with a secret that changed all her plans. The bigger the secret, the more the moments of happiness and anxiety alternate. In addition, there is embarrassment and fear: How can I explain this to anyone? But instead of withdrawing, Mary "set out and went with haste to a Judean town in the hill country, where she entered the house of Zechariah and greeted Elizabeth. When Elizabeth heard Mary's greeting, the child leaped in her womb" (Lk 1:39–41).

Nor did Elizabeth remain focused on herself. She did not talk about what was filling her heart, that the Lord had given her a child in her old age. Her eyes turned toward Mary. Filled with the Holy Spirit, she exclaimed: "Blessed are you among women, and blessed is the fruit of your womb. And why has this happened to me, that the mother of my Lord comes to me? For as soon as I heard the sound of your greeting, the child in my womb leaped for joy. And blessed is she who believed that there would be fulfillment of what was spoken to her by the Lord" (Lk 1:39–46).

Mary remained three months in the house of Elizabeth and her dumbstruck husband. The happy meeting of the two women is described by Luke in fast motion and with many echoes of scenes from the Old Testament. It is a meeting of mutual and wondering respect. It leads to a song of praise to God who is pleased to make the small and simple ones great.

"Mary, God's servant
who had conceived Jesus,
set out immediately for Elizabeth's house
to perform for her the work of a
    servant.
Mary's humility became love in
    action....
The child in Elizabeth's womb
leapt for joy in her body.... Immediately the
mother of the Lord,
full of joy and gratitude, sang the Magnificat
as a song of praise to the Lord.
We too could be servants of the Lord who set
    out immediately,
who cross the hills of difficulties
to serve the Lord with all our heart."

(Mother Teresa)

3 Mary and Simeon

Shortly after his birth, his parents brought Jesus to the temple to consecrate him to the Lord. There an old man named Simeon came up to them. He blessed the parents and said to Mary: "This child is destined for the falling and the rising of many in Israel, and to be a sign that will be opposed so that the inner thoughts of many will be revealed — and a sword will pierce your own soul too" (Lk 2:34–35).

Shortly after the birth, when thoughts are focused on hope and the future, Simeon prophesies that the child will not have an easy road. For some, Jesus will be a stumbling block, while others will be built up, thanks to him. And to the mother he announces that a sword will wound her heart.

This "sword" means that she will share in the growing rejection experienced by Jesus during his public life.

This "sword" is called powerlessness. The mother must look on as her Son approaches extreme danger, without being able to intervene to help.

This "sword" is above all the terrible experience that her Son, who is not even forty years old, is suffering and will be put to death, even though he is innocent.

The wise Simeon insinuates to Mary and to us that God's thoughts are not our thoughts.

God is not someone who guarantees an easier or pain-free life. He does not do this for Jesus. Or for Mary. Or for us and our loved ones. That is hard to understand. Mary will hardly have understood Simeon's words, but she kept them in her heart.

God's ways are mysterious, even for one who believes in his love.

Sometimes we need people like Simeon who preserve us from false expectations, people who allow us to imagine that God can meet us, perhaps in the very experience of harsh reality, in the experience of our limitations.

4 At a Wedding (I)

Bridal Couple in Need

Mary, Jesus and his disciples had been invited to a wedding in Cana. "When the wine gave out, the mother of Jesus said to him, 'They have no wine.' And Jesus said to her, 'Woman, what concern is that to you and to me? My hour has not yet come.' His mother said to the servants, 'Do whatever he tells you.' Now standing there were six stone water jars…. Jesus said to them, 'Fill the jars with water.' And they filled them up to the brim. He said to them, 'Now draw some out, and take it to the chief steward.' So they took it. The steward tasted the water that had become wine…. Jesus did this, the first of his signs, in Cana of Galilee, and revealed his glory; and his disciples believed in him" (Jn 2:1–11).

Mary said to Jesus, "They have no wine." While merely a guest at the wedding, Mary was aware of everything. She recognized the delicate situation, one that was extremely awkward for the bridal couple.

Mary *sees*. She sees what others need. Have others also seen?

Mary *acts*. She makes the problem her own and spells it out: "They have no wine," she says to Jesus.

"Mary, in Cana you noticed that the
wine was running out.
You also know what we are lacking,
what we are suffering from.
You know our needs and our desires;
you know what moves us.
Speak to your Son about our times,
for he is the hope of our future."

(John Paul II)

"Mother, when you see
that my wine is running low —
there are so many mouths,
and there will always be more
that are thirsty and want to be served —
then ask your Son
that the water from my springs
may be like wine and create a thirst
for the fountain of life, for Christ your Son."

(Helder Camara)

5 At a Wedding (II)

"Do Whatever He Tells You"

Jesus' mother said to the servants: "Do whatever he tells you." Jesus refused his mother's request: "Woman, what concern is that to you and to me. My hour has not yet come."

Mary did not give up in the face of this distancing on the part of her Son. She trusted that he would help. As if he were already at work, she said to the servants: "Do whatever he tells you."

Jesus agreed to his mother's request. He did what Mary wanted, but in the way the Father wanted: at *his* time and in *his* manner. He helped not merely because of the embarrassment; he responded with the generosity of God. His help went beyond the need. He changed the water not just into wine, but into especially "good" wine, and not just the amount needed, but in abundance.

The request and faith of his mother prompt Jesus to perform his first public sign.

"When the wine was running short in Cana,
you said:
'Do whatever he tells you.'
Speak these words to us, too, mother
   of Christ.
Help us in our day to understand your Son,
even when his words are hard and
   demanding.
Where shall we go?
You alone have words of eternal life.
The Gospel gives joy and salvation,
but it demands effort and pain.
Help us, mother,
to carry the Gospel in our heart today,
difficult though it may be,
as we await the tomorrow
to which Christ invites us."

(John Paul II)

6 Mary and John

Mary appears only twice in John's Gospel but during very important moments in the life of Jesus. She is at the wedding in Cana, where he performed "the first of his signs" by which he "revealed his glory." Then she is at the crucifixion, the last and greatest "sign," the sign of how much God loved the world. Both times Mary is linked in a network of relationships with Jesus and the disciples. In both texts she is not referred to by name, but rather as the "mother of Jesus," or "his mother."

"Meanwhile, standing near the cross of Jesus were his mother, and his mother's sister, Mary the wife of Clopas, and Mary Magdalene. When Jesus saw his mother and the disciple whom he loved standing beside her, he said to his mother, 'Woman, here is your son.' Then he said to the disciple, 'Here is your mother.' And from that hour the disciple took her into his own home" (Jn 19:25–27). The paths of Mary and the disciple whom Jesus loved, cross. Since both had come into contact with Jesus, they had also come into contact with each other and remained beneath the cross. "When Jesus saw his mother and the disciple whom he loved standing beside her," he instructed them to continue to remain together.

Jesus' departure from this world created yet another new link.

John took Mary in and cared for her as a son cares for his mother: Mary is the one welcomed. John was entrusted to Mary: Mary is the one who welcomes.

Countless people call Mary "mother" as a matter of course, the same way a child says "Mama." Like John, they have taken Mary to themselves, into their life. And Mary has entered their life. As mother. As mother of her crucified and risen Son, who lives in those who are his own, who lives in us, who sometimes suffers and perhaps also grows. The mother of Jesus is also our mother.

"Mary is my mother.
I've never found it hard
to talk to her."

(Mother Teresa)

7 In the Upper Room

After Jesus' death the apostles remain in an upper room in Jerusalem, "devoting themselves to prayer, together with certain women, including Mary the mother of Jesus, as well as his brothers" (Acts 1:14). It is the prelude to Pentecost (2:1–13) when the Holy Spirit comes down upon all who are there. The promise comes true: "I will take you from the nations.... A new heart I will give you, and a new spirit I will put within you; and I will remove from your body the heart of stone and give you a heart of flesh. I will put my spirit within you, and make you follow my statutes.... You shall be my people and I will be your God" (Ezek 36:24–28).

Through the work of the Spirit there is formed a community "driven by enthusiasm for the plan God has in mind for humankind" (Gerhard Lohfink). Mary, the mother of Jesus, is there too. As a sister in a community where all — despite the diversity of offices and ministries — are brothers and sisters. As one who has experienced in her own body what God's Spirit can do. As one who, in the power of the Spirit, listened to God and believed his word.

Mary is and remains an elder sister in the community of Jesus' disciples. She is and at the same time remains a mother. She is and remains the one who says to us by her life: See what God's Spirit can do. Be enthusiastic about the plan God has for humankind. "Do whatever Jesus tells you."

"Since the first Pentecost the figure of Mary appears as a figure of the Church. Together with the apostles she was able to understand that through Christ 'the grace of God has appeared, bringing salvation to all' (Tit 2:11)."

(Brother Roger Schutz)

"In the upper room we see Mary in what is for her an unfamiliar role. In the heart of the emerging Church she awaited the new coming of the Holy Spirit.... Perhaps it is reserved for our time to sense something of the wonderful new thing that happened in Mary, who was so closely associated with Christ's redeeming work and the life of his Church."

(Chiara Lubich)

Mary *and* us

four

A New Kind of Relationship

When the crowd told Jesus that his mother and brothers had arrived, he looked at those present and said: "Here are my mother and my brothers. Whoever does the will of God is my brother and sister and mother" (Mk 3:35). Every community is based on the nuclear family. For the Jews, physical relationship also had a religious meaning. Through their ancestors they were linked to Abraham and his faith.

With this saying Jesus lays the foundation for a new community. It is no longer based on existing relationships but on freely made decisions. That is why in this relationship there are no privileges based on ancestry, family membership or the like. There is a single bond that holds all together: doing God's will.

Jesus' saying makes it clear that where the Father is the center, a new network of relationships is created, of which Mary too is part. This is also how she was Jesus' mother: by following the word and will of the Father.

All this is a fruit of the Spirit. Where God's Spirit is at work, community grows. It was that way at the beginning, at Pentecost in the upper room. So it is to this day.

> "Whoever does the will of God
> is my brother and sister and mother."
>
> *(Mk 3:35)*

2 An Attitude of Profound Listening

"**A** woman in the crowd raised her voice and said to Jesus, 'Blessed is the womb that bore you and the breasts that nursed you!' But he said, 'Blessed rather are those who hear the word of God and obey it' " (Lk 11:27–28). The woman from the crowd meant well. Using a common saying she paid homage to the mother who was so fortunate to have such a son. But this expression was not what was on Jesus' mind. Something else was more important to him: Blessed, he says, are those who hear God's word and put it into practice. His mother, as said, is also among these. Mary's life was shaped by God's word. She had a listening heart in which she kept the divine words, applied them and allowed them to grow and become actions.

"**M**ary is portrayed as the model hearer of God's word, as the servant of the Lord who said yes to God's will, as the divinely favored one who is nothing in herself, but is everything through God's loving kindness. Thus Mary is the perfect

example of a person who allows him or herself
to be opened up and gifted by God, of the community of believers, the Church" (*Catechism of
the German Lutheran Church*, 1979).

"Mary lived in an attitude of listening
to what God said to her through the
    angel
and through events in her life.
Such listening,
which continues to live in the memory,
is the only way to avoid frustration … , the
feeling of being a cog in a wheel.
Only such listening
enables us to find our own identity.
Events have a meaning
and can lead to a conversation with
    God
in which we become aware of our
    good fortune and our greatness.
Then we realize
that we are more fortunate
than the prophets and kings
who longed to see but did not see, who
longed to hear but did not hear."

(Carlo Maria Martini)

3 A Strong and Courageous Faith

Mary appears as a courageous woman of strong faith. A woman who is involved in life, for whom faith is no pious otherworldly matter. With all that she has and is, she is intent on God.

"It's good to speak of Mary's prerogatives, but we should not stop at this, and if, in a sermon, we are obliged from beginning to end to exclaim and say: Ah! Ah!, we would grow tired! … For a sermon on the Blessed Virgin to please me and do me any good, I must see her real life, not her imagined life. I'm sure that her real life was very simple. They show her to us as unapproachable, but they should present her as imitable, bringing out her virtues, saying that she lived by faith just like ourselves."

(Thérèse of Lisieux)

In the apostolic letter *Mulieris Dignitatem*, the Pope speaking of women, recalls the figure of Mary, the mother of God, the Theotokos and tells of the extraordinary dignity to which God raises women in Mary. He points out that although all men and women are called to union with God, Mary fulfills this call in a way that is unparalleled. That is why Mary is "the woman"; she represents the entire human race, the prototype of every man and every woman.... Thus, women who live their vocation out to the fullest, with the faith, nobility and love of Mary, can reveal to the Church the "Marian dimension of the life of Christ's disciples."

(Chiara Lubich)

4 A Reversal of Values

In her song of praise to God, the Mighty One who has done great things for her, Mary says: "He has shown strength with his arm; he has scattered the proud in the thoughts of their hearts. He has brought down the powerful from their thrones, and lifted up the lowly; he has filled the hungry with good things, and sent the rich away empty" (Lk 1:51–53).

This is one of the so-called key gospel texts. But doesn't reality present a very different picture? Yes and no.

"In faith Mary was able to see beyond the present to what is yet to come. Even now we can live from this perspective. Its seeds are already present here in history in people like Mary.... To be sure, the powerful continue to triumph, the rich get whatever they want, and oppressors maintain the upper hand. Yet the revolution God has brought about has already really taken place in a sign.... Mary already proclaims the Gospel of the reversal of established values. The new and real value is listening to God, living a simple life of renunciation and poverty for the sake of the kingdom of God. Wherever this begins to happen, faith, hope and joy increase thanks to the many little 'heralds' of the kingdom of God.... Whoever keeps faith alive, remains sensitive to this fact. And so there is growing concern for people living in poverty, for the disenfranchised and marginalized.... Let us regard people as Mary shows us how to do it in the Magnificat.... The important person is not the one who considers him- or herself such, but rather the one who is important in the sight of God."

(Carlo Maria Martini)

Sister of Those Who Are Tested

"No woman has been chiseled in stone,
carved in wood,
or painted on canvas as often as you —
but always in the radiant bloom of youth.
Dear Mary, didn't you ever get grey
    hair or wrinkles on your face?
Is it really true that you had no
    worries?"

(Pinchas Lapide, in a letter to Mary)

"People have asked me, Mary,
if I could beg you
to put in a good word with the Father
that the roses might lose their thorns.
Forgive me, mother,
for only now do I understand
that the thorns are
an essential part of the rose,
just as suffering
is an essential part of life."

(Helder Camara)

"Mary is not just a distant constellation situated overhead; she is the small and inconspicuous one who is led by God through the darkness of faith and the night of incomprehension. She is truly with us.

"In no other person in the communion of faith have so many taken refuge, those who have come to know themselves as sinners ... as over-burdened and weak.

"She is no substitute for her Son, the only one who can sustain and support us. But just as we all bring one another to Jesus, bear witness to Jesus ... just as we can all become God's mother to each other in faith (see Mk 3:35), so she is the one who through her faith and love, through the word living and lived in her, is mother and companion to us.

"Whenever I think about her, I have more courage to come to grips with God's word, but also courage not to get bogged down in my failures and half measures."

(Klaus Hemmerle)

Mother for All

"Mary is our mother.
Every man and woman without
  exception,
whether a believer or an unbeliever,
is her child,
because her divine Son died for all
and gave her to all as mother."

(Edith Stein)

"I think of the people
who have forgotten the *Ave Maria*,
who consider it ridiculous to call upon you.
I think of the people
who look at your image
with indifference and contempt....
Are they unfortunate?
You are mother of the unfortunate.
Are they sinners?
You are the refuge of sinners.
Have they turned their back on God?
You are the gate of heaven."

(Helder Camara)

"Mother of the deceived,
  pray for us.
Mother of the betrayed,
Mother of those arrested at night,
Mother of those thrown in prison,
Mother of the frightened,
Mother of miners shot dead,
Mother of shipyard workers,
Mother of those interrogated,
Mother of innocent convicts,
Mother of workers,
Mother of students,
Mother of cheaters,
Mother of the truthful,
Mother of the incorruptible,
Mother of the indomitable,
Mother of orphans,
Mother of those who have lost their job,
Mother of mothers who weep,
Mother of fathers who are worried,
  pray for us."

*(Jerzy Popieluszko, Polish priest who was
murdered in 1984)*

Looking at Jesus with Mary

Probably the greatest joy we can give Mary is to look at Jesus with her and follow him as she did. Does she get less than her due in the process? Who could possibly think that her Son would forget her?

"Mary teaches us
to belong totally to Jesus,
to love him alone, to recognize him
when he hides in suffering,
to touch him and to serve him."

(Mother Teresa)

(Mary says):
"You are worried
about how you should honor me.
You must know
that every praise of my Son
is praise of me.
Whoever honors him, honors me.

I have loved him so deeply
and he has loved me so deeply
that we are both, as it were, one heart."

(Birgitta of Sweden)

"In meditating on the life of Mary
in all its phases,
we learn what it means
to live for and with Christ
in our everyday life,
in an objectivity that lacks
excessive excitement yet experiences
    complete intimacy.
Contemplating Mary's life we submit,
even in the darkness that is imposed on
    our faith.
Yet we learn
that we must always be prepared
should Jesus suddenly ask something of
    us.
We find our solemn and major concern
in Mary's attitude,
but as part of something much greater:
her Son's concern that God's name
be glorified on earth
and that his kingdom come ... "

(Hans Urs von Balthasar)

Sources

P. 11: Klaus Hemmerle, in: Karlheinz Collas (Editor), *Hirtenbriefe* (Aachen: Einhard 1994), p. 61.

P. 15: Klaus Hemmerle, in: Rudolf Ammann (Editor), *Sicht-Kontakt. Mit Maria im Gespräch* (Kevelaer: Butzon & Bercker 1988), p. 30.

P. 16: Pope Paul VI., *Marialis cultus,* 2 February1974, #37.

P. 19: Leonardo Boff, *Mensch geworden.* Translated by Malina Höpfner (Freiburg im Breisgau: Herder Verlag 1988), p. 11.

P. 19: Mutter Teresa, *Gedanken für jeden Tag* (Munich: Verlag Neue Stadt 2002), p. 36.

P. 21: Albino Luciani, talk given on 6 August 1978.

P. 22: Martin Luther, *WA* 45; 10,25/26.

P. 23: Jean-Paul Sartre, *Bariona oder der Sohn des Donners. Ein Weihnachtsspiel* (Reinbek: Rowohlt 2001), p. 66f.

P. 27: Romano Guardini, *Die Mutter des Herrn. Ein Brief und ein Entwurf,* 2 (Mainz: Matthias-Grünewald-Verlag), p. 36f. (All rights are with the Katholische Akademie.)

P. 29: Carlo Maria Martini, talk given on 12 January 1982.

P. 30: Hans Urs von Balthasar, *Wenn ihr nicht werdet wie dieses Kind* (Freiburg im Breisgau: Johannes Verlag 1998), p. 53.

P. 32: First par: Romano Guardini, op. cit., p. 39f. Second par: ibid., p. 47.

P. 36: Chiara Lubich, *Maria. Mutter — Schwester — Vorbild* (Munich: Verlag Neue Stadt 2004), p. 27.

P. 38: Carlo Carretto, *Gib mir deinen Glauben* (Freiburg im Breisgau: Herder Verlag 1996), p. 87 f.

P. 43: Mutter Teresa, op. cit., p. 54.

P. 47: Helder Camara, *Maria — eine Mutter auf meinem Weg* (Munich: Verlag Neue Stadt 1985), p. 44.

P. 53: Chiara Lubich, *Alle sollen eins sein* (Munich: Verlag Neue Stadt 1995), p. 241.

P. 59: Carlo Maria Martini, *Lernen von Maria* (Munich: Verlag Neue Stadt 1989), p. 36f.

P. 60: Thérèse of Lisieux, *Last Conversations* (Washington, DC: ICS Publications 1977), p. 161.

P. 61: Chiara Lubich, *Essential Writings* (Hyde Park, NY: New City Press, 2007), p. 200.

P. 63: Carlo Maria Martini, *Marias Lobgesang. Besinnung auf das Magnifikat* (Munich: Verlag Neue Stadt 2003), p. 40-42.

P. 64: Helder Camara, op. cit., p. 79.

P. 66: Helder Camara, op. cit., p. 29.

P. 69: Hans Urs von Balthasar, in: Bischöfliches Ordinariat Rottenburg: *Marienlob in Gebet und Gesang*, Rottenburg 1988.

Also available in the same series: